RISK TA

DANGER
AND
DEDICATION

RISKTAKERS

DANGER AND DEDICATION

LINDA FINLAYSON

CF4•K

For my nephews
John, Jeffrey, Jonathan,
David, Philip, Christopher.

10 9 8 7 6 5 4 3 2 1
© Copyright 2010 Linda Finlayson
Christian Focus Publications
ISBN: 978-1-84550-587-5

Published by Christian Focus Publications,
Geanies House, Fearn, Tain, Ross-shire,
IV20 1TW, Scotland, U.K.
www.christianfocus.com
E-mail: info@christianfocus.com

Cover design by Daniel van Straaten
Cover illustration by Neil Reed

Character and chapter illustrations by Neil Reed
Maps by Fred Apps
Printed and bound by Norhaven AS, Denmark

CONTENTS

LET'S GET STARTED

Risks are all around us. In everyday life we take risks with most things we do. We could slip in the bath, find ourselves in a car crash or eat food in a restaurant that wasn't properly prepared. All of those things would be called accidents. They certainly aren't planned events.

Athletes take risks as they train for their sport. Snowboarders or skiers push themselves to try more and more difficult manoeuvres until they master them, but they don't do it foolishly. They work up to the more difficult things slowly, and they keep their bodies fit to be able to withstand the rigours of their sport.

None of these are 'a venture undertaken without regard to the possibility of suffering harm, loss or danger.' They are part of everyday living or part of preparation for a sport. A venture is more like taking a gamble or a risk, only thinking about what you can get in return for exposing yourself to unnecessary danger.

Maybe you've taken some silly risks without thinking about the danger. Something like accepting a dare to eat something really disgusting just to show you can, even though it could make you ill. Or going to a dangerous place just to prove you're brave. Those are foolish risks.

Maybe you know of someone who likes to try the more extreme sports or perform dangerous stunts. But they do them on the spur of the moment, rather than taking time to prepare properly for them. They take those risks, not because they want to excel at something, but because they like the thrill or adrenaline rush they get. When we are faced with a dangerous situation our bodies begin pumping adrenaline which gives a surge of energy and excitement. Some people like that feeling so much they do more and more dangerous things to keep the adrenaline pumping, and take no thought for safety. Very foolish indeed.

So when is it a good thing to take a risk? Learning new things always comes with a risk, like learning to drive a car. But you don't just start driving without having studied the rules of the road or having an instructor. Meeting new people can be risky because we don't know if they will be good friends or not. But these things are still good risks, especially because we do them carefully.

In this book we will learn about people who took good risks. They chose to take a risk, not for the thrill, not to prove something to anyone else, but to obey God. Jesus warned his disciples that following him was not an easy thing. Christians can expect to be persecuted, beaten, put in prison and even risk death. But for all of that risk, Jesus promised that he would be with his followers, giving them strength and courage, as well as a wonderful home in heaven. Now that's something worth taking a risk for, don't you think?

Come on an adventure now and read about heroes from long ago and in recent time who took such risks. Follow one man as he outruns the king's spies, another who bravely goes into a despotic king's presence, someone who escapes a murderous crowd, another who endures prison, and finally two Bible characters who obeyed God and risked their lives for Him. These are the kind of risks that God asked of those who love him.

Are you that kind of person?

WILLIAM TYNDALE

William Tyndale was born in England near the Welsh border around 1494. He was educated at Oxford, and by the age of twenty-one he knew eight different languages. William was ordained as a priest and became a tutor to the household of Sir John Welsh. William's greatest desire was to translate the Bible into English so that everyone in the country could read God's Word for themselves. However, King Henry VIII, his advisors, and some church officials thought otherwise. They thought the Bible should only be read by church leaders in Latin, and then they would explain God's Word to the people. So William decided to work secretly on his translation of the Bible. But where could he do that in safety if the King and the church leaders were watching him? Friends smuggled William out of England to the European continent. Over the next ten years William moved from place to place, outrunning agents of the King and church who searched everywhere for him to put him in prison. During that time, William was able to translate the entire New Testament and write several books, all of which were smuggled back into England for people to read. This only fuelled the anger of the King, who redoubled his efforts to find William Tyndale and put an end to his life.

GOD'S SECRET AGENT

(1535-36)

A quiet voice urged William, 'this way,' as he followed his guide through the winding streets of Antwerp. The sun had set a while ago and the gathering shadows made it difficult to see the way. William, shifting his small trunk of books and papers in his arms, was glad he wasn't alone in this Belgium city.

William had met the young man sent by an English merchant, Thomas Poyntz, near the city gates earlier in the day, but they had waited until now to creep into the city. A printer had recently been arrested for printing copies of Protestant literature. No one was quite sure who had informed on him. So they weren't taking any chances.

After a few more darkening streets, the guide led William to the river's edge.

'The third house along,' the young man said. 'Mr. Poyntz lives there. It's all right here. You'll be safe.'

William hesitated at first, as the young man slipped away into the night. After so many years of hiding, could he really live in a house and sleep in a bed like everyone else? God had protected him the last ten years, allowing him to finish translating all of the New Testament and the first five books of the Old. But he never had a place to settle, where it was safe to go out in daylight hours. He would spend his days poring over the Greek and Latin texts of the Bible and searching for just the right words to translate them into English. Then he arranged to have his translations printed. That was dangerous because it was against the law. Finding a printer who was willing to risk the punishment was difficult. More than once William's printers had been caught and questioned, forcing William to run for his life before the soldiers found him too.

Had he now found a safe place?

William hitched up the small trunk and walked down to the house.

The door opened immediately. Thomas, a prosperous looking English merchant, dressed in a green doublet that hung to his knees over brown hose, and a fur lined coat, welcomed him. 'Come in, come in, my friend,' he said with a smile.

William, dressed in a priest's simple black robe, stepped through the door into a brightly lit room with a fire burning warmly in a stone fireplace.

'Are you sure this is a good idea?' William asked anxiously. 'What about your safety, and your family?'

'This area of Antwerp belongs to us merchants. The local officials will not interfere with anyone who lives here. You have been in hiding too long. You need someone to take care of you. My wife will soon see to fattening you up.' Thomas laughed as he patted his own rounded tummy that bulged a little over his belt.

William sighed with relief. A number of English merchants had settled in the city, bringing trade and wealth to the area. The city officials wanted them to stay. So they had offered the merchants their own area to live in and do as they pleased.

If only some of William's other friends had found such safety. Over the years the king's spies had caught others who were also writing Christian books to encourage those of the reformed faith. In their books, they spoke out about the wrong things that some of the church leaders were teaching. So they had been arrested and killed. It made William very sad when he thought of them.

'There is one thing you must remember, William,' Thomas added as he showed his guest the room set aside for him. 'You are free to walk about the streets in this part of the city only. If you leave the English merchant area you may well be arrested and I would have difficulty helping you.'

William nodded absently. He was looking about the chamber, pleased to see a large table set by a window, a perfect place to lay out his books and writing materials. A bed stood against the opposite wall, along with a large chest to store his meagre collection of clothing. 'This room is wonderful. So bright and pleasant after the hovels I've had to hide in over the years.'

Thomas smiled at his enthusiasm and was glad he could use his wealth to help, but he worried that William had not really listened to what he had said. And sure enough, a few weeks later Thomas had to remind him again.

William had arrived back at the merchant's house while the evening meal was being served. As he entered he saw the Poyntz family assembled at the wooden trestle table, already enjoying a thick stew in bread trenchers. William made his apologies for being late as Thomas invited him to take a place at the table. Mrs. Poyntz called the maid to prepare a trencher for William.

'Where have you been, my friend?' Thomas inquired. 'I was concerned when I didn't find you in your chamber busy with your books.'

William shook his head. 'I don't study on Saturdays. Don't forget I'm also a minister and I must do some pastoral work. There are many in the city who need comfort and assurance in these difficult times.'

Thomas was concerned. 'Yes, I understand, but you preach every Sunday when we gather for worship in people's homes. Isn't that enough? You really need to be careful when you are about the city streets.'

'Don't worry, Thomas,' William assured him. 'I'll be careful. This is excellent food,' he added between mouthfuls.

Thomas' wife smiled, glad to see her house guest eating well. Then Thomas asked, 'How's your revision of the New Testament coming along? Have you corrected all the printing errors yet?'

'Just about. And I've also been looking at some of the English words I had used and changing some of them to make the Biblical passages clearer. It's a lot of work, but this edition will be easier to read.'

'Excellent,' Thomas replied. 'Then I will let our friend know he should get his printing press ready.'

Once the new edition was printed, the merchants began to bundle up the books and hide them in sacks of grain and other goods. The sacks were loaded onto

the merchant ships and sent on their way to London. The merchants who received the sacks in England carefully removed the books before selling the goods. Then they secretly passed out the Bibles to those who longed to read God's Word for themselves. However, some of the copies were found by the Bishop of London.

'How did these Bibles get into England?' the Bishop demanded of one of his spies.

The man shook his head, stepping back to avoid being hit by the Bible the Bishop threw at him.

'Get out there and buy up all the Bibles you can find and burn them. I want England purged of these wretched translations!'

His servant fled from the room to obey his master's instructions. But the Bishop knew he couldn't burn all the copies. The only way to stop people from reading the Bible in English was to stop the man who was translating them. So he began to make a clever plan.

After a year in Antwerp, William was much healthier and still enjoying Thomas Poyntz's hospitality. In fact the generous allowance that Thomas gave him made it possible for William to help those who had fled from England to avoid persecution. They didn't have wealthy friends like Thomas Poyntz, so William took the money he was given and gave it to his fellow Christians who were poor and in need of food. In this way many of them managed to survive.

One day as William was visiting a poor widow, he was approached by a handsome young man. William didn't notice him at first, because he stood respectfully out of the way as William had gone into the widow's cottage. When he came out, the young man was still there.

'Mr. Tyndale?' the young man asked.

William was immediately on his guard. Anyone asking after him was usually a spy or at least someone who would betray him to the authorities.

The young man didn't wait for a reply before explaining himself. 'I'm a student at the University in Louvain, not far from here. I rode over to meet with some reformed Christians and I've lost the directions. Someone over there pointed you out to me and said you would know how to find them.'

William hesitated, studying the young man's face. He looked genuine, but after so many years of hiding from spies, William didn't know who to trust anymore. 'Where are you staying?' he asked.

The young man pointed to an inn at the end of the street. 'My name is Henry Phillips,' he said. 'Would you like to share a meal with me at the inn? I have some questions about something I read in the Bible. Maybe you could explain it to me?'

William had finished his visits for the day, so he agreed to go with Henry. Maybe if they talked about the Bible, William could decide if Henry was really interested or just pretending.

William was surprised and pleased to discover that Henry had indeed read the English Bible and had some very good questions. They spent several hours at the inn discussing the doctrines found in parts of Paul's letters.

When William arrived back at the Poyntz home, he was excited to tell Thomas about his new friend. 'He is a student and a very able one. He's sincerely interested in God's Word. I was going to invite him to our worship service but I thought I should tell you first.'

Thomas rubbed his chin, a little worried. 'Are you sure he's not a spy? I don't want to endanger you or our congregation. Why did he just suddenly turn up and seek you out?'

William shrugged. 'I don't know, but I'm sure he's not a spy. Meet him for yourself,' William urged. 'See what you think.'

'Hmmmm...I suppose we could invite him over for a meal. Ask him to come on Monday and we'll see if he's genuine.'

On Monday, Henry bowed graciously to Thomas and presented Mrs. Poyntz with a bouquet of wildflowers. There were smiles all round as the young man told them stories of his fellow students and professors. And then they all became serious as they began to discuss a particular passage from Romans that Henry said he still didn't fully understand.

After he left, Thomas said, 'Well, he's certainly a personable young man, and as you said, has a grasp of Christian doctrine. I guess it will be safe to let him into our little congregation.'

And so Henry became a part of the English group that met every Sunday to worship God. He even began to accompany William on his pastoral visits to the poor of Antwerp, taking advantage of the time they walked between houses to ask more questions about the Bible. He appeared to be hungry to learn as much of God's Word as he could.

One day in May, after spending the morning with William, Henry suggested that they stop at an inn for a meal. 'I know a very good place,' he said. 'It's over on the next street. If we go through this passageway here we can take a shortcut.' Henry stepped back to let William go first.

William smiled at his friend and started down the narrow stone passage between two houses. But as he came to the end he saw two soldiers waiting there. William started to turn around to run to safety, but Henry was right behind him. There was no room to get around the young man. William was caught between Henry and the soldiers.

'You're not getting away this time,' said Henry with a grim smile. 'Soldier, this is William Tyndale. Arrest him!'

William looked at Henry in disbelief as the soldiers began to fasten chains to his wrists. Henry's face flushed red.

'I had to do it,' he said bitterly. 'I had no money. The Bishop paid all my debts, gave me clothes and told me to find you. I had no choice.'

William said nothing, but Henry knew very well there was always a choice between right and wrong, however difficult. As the soldiers led William away Henry decided to go to the inn himself. He was going to drink a large tankard of ale, even if he didn't really feel like celebrating.

William, still bound with chains, was thrust into a wooden cage on a large wagon. The rough wood hurt his back as the wagon bumped along the road. He knew where they were taking him. Vilvoorde Castle. Other reformers had been captured and put there, only to waste away and die in the terrible dungeons. William began to pray, asking God for courage to face the imprisonment. He wasn't angry or even very surprised at finally becoming a prisoner after all those years of running and hiding. He knew that at sometime he would very likely be killed for his defiance of the king and church leaders. And he also knew that he would do it all over again. Nothing was more important than God's Word, and God had allowed him the privilege of translating it into English. Now anyone in England who had a desire to read God's Word could do so.

Devotional Thought:

God is our refuge and strength, a very present help in trouble.

Psalm 46:1

William might well have remembered this verse as he sat in that dark, damp dungeon. God was his refuge or safe place. William could go to God with his fears, worries and pain and know that God would give him the strength to carry on. And notice the second half of the verse: God is a 'very present help in trouble.' 'Very present' is there to emphasise that God's help is right there when we need it. And it comes at the right time, when we are in the middle of troubles and difficulties. None of us are likely to have to go to prison for serving God as William did, but there are just as many other times where we need God's help. There might be difficult situations in our family, our school or our neighbourhood that God knows all about. He is the safe place we can run to in prayer and he will give us strength and help to meet those difficulties.

William was kept in prison for eighteen months. At his trial some church leaders lectured him on how wrong he was to defy the laws of the king who had prohibited an English Bible. William remained strong even when the judge sentenced him to death by strangulation and burning. He counted it all joy to suffer for God.

Just before he died, William prayed out loud for all to hear. 'Lord, open the King of England's eyes.' And God answered William's prayer. Just three years later, King Henry decided to lift the ban on the translation of the English Bible. And not only that. He passed a law that said every church must have an English Bible on display, available to anyone who wished to read it. God, who is greater than any king, can change a king's heart.

BELGIUM

FACT FILE

Belgium is a beautiful west European country that is bordered by France, Netherlands and the North Sea. Brussels is the capital of Belgium and the currency is the Euro. Belgium experiences mild winters and cool summers. It is famous for its medieval castles and gothic cathedrals. Antwerp has the fourth largest seaport in the world, located on the right bank of the river Scheldt, which is linked to the North Sea by the estuary Westerschelde. Antwerp is also one of the famous art cities of Belgium. The other popular art cities are Bruges and Ghent.

Belgium is both multicultural and multilingual. The official languages of Belgium are French, German and Dutch.

After World War II, Belgium played an important role in laying the foundation for the European Community. Today, Brussels, the capital of Belgium, is also the capital of the European Union (EU). Brussels is also the Headquarters of NATO (North Atlantic Treaty Organisation).

Northern Europe in the 1500s

ADONIRAM JUDSON

Adoniram Judson lived from 1788–1850. He was born in Massachusetts in the United States. His father was a minister and Adoniram grew up hearing the gospel. He was converted at age twenty-one. From the time of his conversion he was convinced God had called him to be a missionary. However, no missionaries had ever been sent from America, so there was no missionary society to help him. That didn't stop Adoniram. He and several other young men all joined together to ask the churches to send them to Burma, and the first American Missionary Society was established.

Meanwhile Adoniram had met and married Ann Hasseltine. He told her right from the beginning that his life's work was in Burma, on the other side of the world. Because the only transportation at that time was by boat, he couldn't promise that once they left America they would ever return. Burma was not a friendly place. Only one missionary had ever managed to stay in that country. All others had been driven out by persecution or disease. Ann never hesitated. She too felt the call to be a missionary, even in such a dangerous place.

They arrived in the city of Rangoon in Burma in 1813, and preached for five years before anyone was converted to Christianity. Once the new converts began to tell others, then the difficulties began.

BEFORE THE
GOLDEN FEET

(1820-1823)

Adoniram and Ann jogged along on their horses early one bright, hot morning, just outside the city of Rangoon. As they rode along the dirt road that was shaded by tall teak and acacia trees they could hear the monkeys chattering in the branches and the distant sound of the Buddhist temple bells chiming in the breeze. Adoniram breathed in the aroma of the rhododendron shrubs as he turned to smile at his wife. They had lived in Burma for five difficult years and now suddenly it seemed that it was getting easier. Just then some men stepped out in front of them, causing the horses to rear with fright.

Adoniram looked down at the men, puzzled at the sudden appearance of the Buddhist priests, with their shaved heads and traditional yellow gowns. The head teacher stepped forward and shouted at them.

'You may not come down this road!'

'Why?' Adoniram asked. 'We ride down this road most mornings to bathe in the mineral springs.'

'No more!' came the harsh reply. 'The Viceroy has passed a law. No foreigners may ride or walk within a half mile of the sacred grounds of our great pagodas.' He waved a piece of paper at them.

The Judsons didn't argue. They turned their horses around and rode back to the mission house in silence. But Adoniram was not silent when they reached home.

They found the Colemans, the other missionary couple living at the mission house, and told them about the incident. 'Those Buddhist priests are stirring up trouble again,' Adoniram said. 'It's all because we finally have a few people who have converted from Buddhism to Christianity. The priests are feeling threatened, worried that we will persuade more people to become Christians.'

James Coleman agreed. 'They have been threatening our newest convert, Maung Shway-gnong, saying they will get the Viceroy to bring charges against him and any others who forsake their native religion.'

'But what can we do?' Ann asked. 'We've been careful to obey the laws. You built the zayat and invited people to come in rather than trying to preach in the streets or their homes. Will the Viceroy even stop you translating the Bible into the Burmese language?'

'I think we need to go to the Emperor,' Adoniram replied, always willing to face a problem head on. 'If we can appeal to the new king, he might agree to give us freedom to preach and teach. Then the Viceroy and the Buddhist priests couldn't stop us.'

'True,' James replied, slowly. 'But the Emperor could also have us killed. Remember when he became king a few months ago? He killed five hundred soldiers who were loyal to his father.'

'That's a risk we have to take.' Adoniram looked at his wife, who nodded slowly.

'Yes,' she replied. 'You should go.'

And so the preparations began for the long trip. The men had a boat built specially to carry everything and everyone: the rowers and their head man, the cook, their luggage, some weapons and themselves. Travelling up the wide Irrawaddy River was dangerous. Along with all the usual travellers and merchants selling their wares, were pirates, who attacked people and stole whatever they could. There were also crocodiles, snakes and other dangers to watch for.

Adoniram also needed a gift to give the Emperor. No one came into the Golden Presence, as he was called, without a precious gift for him.

'I think we should give him a Bible,' Adoniram said. 'It's the most precious thing we own.'

'Yes,' James agreed, 'but it needs to be very special looking. Why don't we get a craftsman to cover it in gold leaf?'

So it was agreed. While the boat was being built, the gift was prepared by a craftsman. Several weeks later the men kissed their wives goodbye, and stepped aboard the long narrow boat that was to be their home for the next month as they sailed up the enormous Irrawaddy River to the city of Ava, the home of the Emperor King Bagyidaw.

In the first few weeks they passed rice fields and then forested plains full of fragrant fruit trees. Villages of bamboo huts dotted the shores of the wide river. At night they tied up their boat at a village's wooden dock so the rowing crew could sleep. Someone always had to stand guard, in case they were attacked by pirates. As the river narrowed, they passed abandoned cities, where kings had once lived, with towering white stone pagodas and carved Buddha statues. Only the poor and disabled lived near what had once been thriving cities. Adoniram's heart ached for the people and their spiritual blindness.

They were unhappy and forgotten, even though they were surrounded by the statues of their gods.

Once they arrived at the city of Ava, Adoniram and James put on their white gowns to show they were religious teachers. The gowns were similar to the yellow gowns the Buddhist priests wore, but they had chosen a different colour so that the Emperor would know that the missionaries were a different kind of religious teacher.

As they approached the palace Adoniram was amazed by its beauty. Inside and out was covered with gold. The golden columns in all the rooms had intricate patterns and even the floors were gold. They left their shoes outside and followed the official through room after room of rich teak furniture and flowing curtains. Once they arrived at the audience chamber, the official instructed them on what to do.

'When the Golden Feet arrives, you must fall to the floor and stay there until you are commanded to rise,' he said. 'You may never look at the Golden Eyes, even when he speaks to you. Otherwise he may become very angry.'

Adoniram and James nodded, taking their place at the front of court, near the golden throne. Then all at once, everyone in the large chamber fell to the floor in a fluttering of gowns. Quickly Adoniram and James knelt down, put their hands together and bowed deeply.

The Emperor, dressed in a long robe and carrying a large sword, entered and took his place on the throne. He called for his advisor to tell him what these foreigners were doing in his palace.

'We are teachers, Great King,' Adoniram replied, not waiting for the advisor to speak.

'You speak Burmese?' King Bagyidaw asked, surprised and forgetting to be angry that the foreigners had spoken out of turn. 'Are you teachers of religion?'

'Yes, Great King, and we wish to share our religion with your people.'

There was silence. The court waited to see what the Emperor would say.

The official handed the Emperor a copy of a tract about God that Adoniram had written for the Burmese people. The Emperor began to read it, but after a few sentences he opened his hand and let the pamphlet fall to the floor. The official then tried to present the gold covered Bible, but King Bagyidaw turned away.

The official spoke to the missionaries. 'The Emperor has no use for your religious book. You may practice your own religion without harm but he doesn't want you talking to his people about it. We have our own religion. You must go now.'

Dejected, Adoniram and James crawled out of the Audience Chamber. They had failed to get royal approval to be missionaries to the Burmese people.

'Being a Christian has just become more dangerous for the Burmese people,' the advisor warned them later. 'You are fortunate that the Emperor only turned his back and didn't order your execution. But now he knows about you and your work and he will be watching.'

When Adoniram and James returned to the mission house in Rangoon, they told their wives and the few Christian Burmese people what had happened.

'We took a risk going to the Emperor and it failed,' James reported. 'We can no longer meet at the zayat or worship publicly. No one will dare ask about Christianity any more.'

Adoniram looked around at the small group of converts. He wondered how soon they would stop coming to worship God and study the scriptures, afraid of being arrested and tortured. He felt discouraged and wondered why he ever thought God had wanted him to come to Burma.

Then Maung Thahlah spoke. 'Christ has taught us to not to fear those who can kill the body only, but to fear him who can destroy both soul and body in hell.'

The other Burmese Christians nodded in agreement. 'We must not stop worshipping the true God. And we must still tell others even though it is dangerous.'

Adoniram was amazed at their courage, but he was still a little doubtful that when persecution came that they would remain strong. Over the next few days, he learned how sure the Burmese Christians were. Not only did they come regularly to attend prayer meetings and study the scriptures, but they began to bring people with them.

Slowly over the next two years the tiny group grew until there were eighteen Christians meeting in the mission house. God protected them and not one of them was arrested. During that time a new Viceroy was appointed and he was not interested in persecuting the Christians. When the Buddhist priests complained to him about the missionaries, he shrugged and told them to leave them alone.

The Colemans decided to leave Burma and Dr. Price and his family arrived in Rangoon to take their place. Dr. Price was an eye specialist and news of his ability to remove cataracts from people's eyes spread quickly. It appeared to the Burmese people that Dr. Price could cure blindness. Even the Emperor came to hear of him and summoned him to appear before the Golden Feet.

When Adoniram heard about this, he offered to go with Dr. Price. He could speak Burmese much better than Dr. Price and he knew what do when appearing before the Emperor. So together the two men set off on the same trip that Adoniram had taken two years before, but this time he didn't bother to take a gift or even dress in special robes.

As the two men knelt on the golden floor with their hands clasped and heads bowed, the Emperor questioned Dr. Price about his medical skills. Whenever Dr. Price needed some help with answering, Adoniram acted as his interpreter. At first the Emperor took no notice of Adoniram. He was much more interested in the doctor and called him back for several more interviews. Then one day King Bagyidaw suddenly spoke to Adoniram.

'Are you a doctor too?' the Emperor asked.

Adoniram realized that the Emperor didn't remember him. 'No,' he replied cautiously. 'I'm a teacher of religion.'

'Do you have any converts?'

Adoniram's heart began to pound. He couldn't lie, but to speak the truth might remind the Emperor that he had forbidden any Burmese people to change their religion. Praying for courage, Adoniram answered, 'Yes, Great King. Some are foreigners like myself and some are Burmese. I preach to them every Sunday.'

'What! In the Burmese language? Let me hear you. Preach to me,' he ordered.

Adoniram could hardly believe his ears. The entire audience room went silent as he prayed for God to give him the right words. Then he began to tell the Emperor that there is only one God, who exists eternally and is the creator of the heavens and the earth. The Emperor listened for a while to Adoniram's sermon on who God is and what he has done for his people. Then abruptly the Emperor told him to stop.

'I want Dr. Price to remain in Ava. There is much medical work he can do here. Mr. Judson you may stay too, if you choose. I will see that you are given land to live on.' Then the two men were dismissed from the Golden Presence.

Adoniram came away dazed. How was it that two years ago the Emperor had threatened the Christians with persecution and now he was inviting missionaries to live in the capital city? True, the Emperor did not want to be a Christian, nor had he changed the order that the Burmese people must not change their religion. But now missionaries were welcome in Ava. Only God could have brought this about. Adoniram felt like singing and shouting. He could hardly wait to return to Rangoon and tell his wife and the Burmese Christians.

Devotional Thought:
The king's heart is a stream of water in the hand of the LORD; he turns it wherever he will.
Proverbs 21:1

Adoniram would have read this verse and nodded his head vigorously. God had changed King Bagyidaw's heart from rejecting the missionaries to accepting them. It was just like engineers today who can change the direction of a stream or river by building a dam or can make a lake by digging a huge hole near a spring or stream. God can change how people think and even their hearts. There is nothing too difficult for God to do.

Adoniram needed to remember that verse often a few years later. When war broke out between England and Burma, King Bagyidaw ordered the arrest of all foreign men, thinking they might be spies for the English. Adoniram was arrested with them and put in a terrible prison for over two years. Adoniram was treated very cruelly. But Adoniram knew that these events were in God's hands too, and he was ordering them to bring glory to God. During that terrible time a number of people were converted through Adoniram's testimony.

Adoniram's wife, Ann, and the Burmese Christians did their best to visit him, bringing him food and encouraging him. Ann went often to the Viceroy, and anyone one else in the government who would listen, to ask for Adoniram's release, and his fellow Christians never stopped praying. After almost two years, Adoniram was set free.

BURMA

FACT FILE

Burma is a country that is located in South East Asia. It was called Burma until its name was changed to Myanmar in 1989. China borders it on the north and northeast while on the east and southeast, it is bordered by Laos and Thailand.

The name 'Myanmar' is derived from the local name Myanma Naingngandaw, which is a name used by the regime which is currently in power there. The population is about 60 million. The main language spoken in the country is Myanmar though English is also widely spoken and understood.

Myanmar is divided into states, divisions, townships, wards and villages. The national currency of Myanmar is Kyat.

In 2006 the capital of Myanmar was moved from Yangon (formerly Rangoon) to Nay Pyi Taw.

Burma in the 1800s

JONATHAN GOFORTH

Jonathan Goforth lived from 1859 to 1936. He was born on a farm in south western Ontario, Canada. He grew up in a Christian home and was converted when he was eighteen. His father sent him to study at Knox College in Toronto, where Jonathan felt God was calling him to go to China. He met Rosalind Bell-Smith at a church prayer meeting and a year later they were married. She also wanted to serve God in China.

Their life in China was not easy. Among other things, many of the Chinese people were suspicious of foreigners, afraid they came with evil plans to hurt or kill people, especially children. So Jonathan and Rosalind decided to have an 'open house to all.' In the town of Changte (now Anyang), they built their mission house in the traditional Chinese style, but with many Western additions: board floors, glass windows with shutters, a cellar, an organ, and a sewing machine. They expected to have a few people come by occasionally, but almost every day hundreds of people came! Jonathan would greet the visitors from his veranda, present the Gospel to them in a sermon, and then offer a tour to one hundred and fifty people at a time. The Goforths were thrilled to have the people come to them, even if it did mean they had very little privacy for their growing family. They hoped that the Chinese people would forget their suspicions about foreigners. But there were some who would not give up their distrust and anger. They thought that missionaries had come to 'invade' their country. That's when life suddenly became very dangerous for the Goforth family.

DELIVERED FROM DEATH

JUNE 1900

A voice sounded loudly from outside the mission house gate, 'I have urgent news!'

'Who are you?' Jonathan Goforth replied from inside.

'I'm a messenger sent from the American Consul in Cheefoo' came the breathless reply.

Jonathan relaxed and opened the gate to a Chinese man. His clothing was torn in places and he had some scrapes and bruises. 'I have news. I should have been here weeks ago, but the gangs of bandits and Boxers are threatening everyone.' He stopped to catch his breath and accept a cup of water. 'You must pack up everything and flee! Head south. The Boxers have already cut off all roads leading north.'

Rosalind had come out of the house in time to hear the messenger's speech. 'Is that why we've had no mail from the mission office or anyone else?'

'Yes, a rebellion is growing and all foreigners must get to safety. At first the Boxers were angry at the government for not helping the people in these times of drought and bad harvests. But now they're blaming all those who aren't Chinese. You really must get away as quickly as you can. They've been killing missionaries and Chinese Christians as they move down from the north.'

Jonathan and Rosalind looked at each other and had the same thought. They must warn the other missionaries in the area. If they didn't move quickly they too might die!

Jonathan had to find carts to carry their four children and items they would need for the journey. It would take several weeks to reach Hankow in the south. Rosalind rushed indoors to start sorting and packing up clothing and bedding.

'Mrs. Cheng,' she called out to the children's nurse. 'Keep all the children inside the house.'

During the next few days, the other missionaries arrived: Mr. and Mrs. Mackenzie, Mr. Griffiths and Dr. Leslie. Together they packed up the carts. Mrs. Cheng kept the older children busy carrying items from the house to the carts.

'We'll look like gypsies travelling through the countryside,' Rosalind remarked as she shoved the last bundle of quilts into a corner of the cart. 'I only wish we could take my organ and sewing machine.'

'That's hardly practical,' Jonathan replied, checking the ropes that held canopies of quilts in place over each cart. Then he noticed the sad look on Rosalind's face and stopped to hug her. 'I know this will be the third time you've lost your home since we've been in China. First a fire, then a flood and now this, but they are, after all, only things.'

'Quite right,' Rosalind agreed, trying to smile. 'I need to remember what's really important. Jesus himself had no place to lay his head when he was here on earth, so why should I fuss over a sewing machine?'

Big strong oxen pulled the creaking carts full of people and their belongings as they waved goodbye to the Chinese Christians lining the road. Jonathan wondered if they would still be here when he returned. *If* he returned. Had God really decided that Jonathan's work in China was over? They had made such good progress. All the villages he had visited recently now had a small group of Christians, hungry to study God's Word. *Please Heavenly Father, protect them*, Jonathan prayed.

The journey was very difficult. They bounced along on springless carts, feeling every bump and hole in the road. The summer sun beat down on them until they felt like they couldn't breathe. They dared not stop under shaded trees or by cool streams. They must keep moving south.

Angry, sullen faces in each village watched them as the carts rumbled through. Some voices even called out, 'Kill, kill.'

Paul, Jonathan's nine-year-old son, huddled close to his father in the cart. 'Will they kill us?' he asked anxiously.

'I haven't stop praying since we left,' Jonathan replied as he put his arm around the boy. 'We're in God's hands. It's the safest place to be.'

At night they had to rest the animals, so they looked for open places to gather the carts around them. A few brave Chinese Christians had given them what food they could spare, but no one dared offer them a place to stay. Jonathan organized a schedule for himself and the other men to watch through the night for bandits or gangs of Boxers. Rosalind held their eight-month-old son close, comforting him as he cried himself to sleep.

A few days of travel took them to the Yellow River where they met a small group of British soldiers also heading south. They agreed to travel with the missionaries. Now everyone felt safer, but it didn't last very long. As they arrived at the walled town of Hsintien, the commander announced they couldn't wait for the slow moving carts. They had to press on.

As the missionaries entered the city, groups of people began to gather around them. 'Keep moving,' Jonathan urged the carters. 'Head for that inn. If they let us stay, we can get a good rest and be safe inside.'

The crowd grew until the oxen had to force their way down the street. Jonathan, seeing that some carried sticks and stones, pulled his daughter, Helen, and son, Paul, close to him, while Rosalind held baby Wallace and little Ruth clung to her nurse, Mrs. Cheng. Then Jonathan had an idea.

'Hold up the baby,' he said to his wife. 'The Chinese love children. Let them see him.'

So Rosalind held Wallace up. She turned back and forth so that the crowd on both sides could see him. But it seemed to have little effect. Their faces were still angry, although no one threw any stones. The Goforths and their party climbed down quickly and hurried into the inn. After much discussion, the innkeeper was persuaded to let them stay, if they paid him all their money. Jonathan didn't hesitate. He knew they still had at least another ten days of travel and they needed rest. He emptied his pockets and handed the innkeeper the money.

The night was hot and noisy. The crowd surrounded the inn and from time to time shouted

threats and threw stones. The Goforths tried to sleep, but it was no use. Finally, Jonathan announced that they needed to pray. He called everyone together and opened his small book *Clarke's Scripture Promises* that he always carried in his pocket. He read out the promises listed for that day.

The eternal God is your dwelling place, and underneath are the everlasting arms. And he thrust out the enemy before you and said, Destroy. [Deuteronomy 32:27]

As for me, I am poor and needy, but the Lord takes thought for me. You are my help and my deliverer; do not delay, O my God! [Psalm 40:17]

So we can confidently say, 'The Lord is my helper; I will not fear; what can man do to me?' [Hebrews 13:6]

'These are God's promises to us,' Jonathan said. 'Now let's pray that he will give us courage and strength to carry on.' They spent the next hour in prayer and then were able to sleep for the rest of the night.

The next morning when Jonathan looked out of the window his heart sank a little. The crowd had not gone away. He pulled back from the window just in time to miss a rock aimed at his head. Forcing a smile, he turned to his wife and children. 'Let's go,' he said. 'I'm sure they'll let us through.' He patted a worried-looking Paul on the shoulder.

Rosalind looked doubtful too, but scooped up baby Wallace and took Helen by the hand. Just then Mrs. Cheng knocked and entered. Little Ruth ran to her nurse and the Chinese woman wrapped her in a warm hug. 'I'll take care of her,' Mrs. Cheng promised.

They joined the others at the carts. The crowd was quiet, watching every move the missionaries made. When it came time to move out the carts, the crowd parted and let them through. Jonathan should have felt glad, but the unnatural silence bothered him. Somehow he knew there would be trouble ahead.

As they pulled out of the city gates, Jonathan almost stopped breathing. Lining the road were several hundred men with arms full of stones, daggers in their belts and other weapons by their sides. He looked back and saw the gates closing behind them. They were trapped! All at once the men began throwing the stones. As they showered down on the carts, everyone huddled under quilts for protection. Then someone fired a gun and the men rushed forward, surrounding the carts.

Jonathan jumped off his cart, waving his arms and shouting in Chinese, 'Take everything, but don't kill.' He had to protect his wife and children.

Almost immediately a fierce group of men turned on him. A man with a broad two-handed sword swung at his neck. The blow sent Jonathan reeling to the side, but when he raised his hand to feel for blood there was none. He must have been hit with the wide part of the sword. He had no time to rejoice, though. The sword swung again, crashing down on his pith helmet, cracking the hat in two, but again no blood. Angry that his efforts had failed to stop the missionary, the rebel called for help. Jonathan was surrounded and could feel blows from all sides. His arm was slashed in several places and he felt terrible pain at the back of his head as someone clubbed him. He staggered, knowing he was losing consciousness. Suddenly he heard a voice clearly saying, 'Fear not! They are praying for you.' Then he heard the sound of a galloping horse...

A short time later Jonathan became aware of his surroundings. He was still lying on the ground where he had fallen. Beside him was an unconscious man and between them and the fighting was a horse kicking furiously at the rebels, protecting Jonathan from their attack. Scrambling to his feet, he stumbled away and into the arms of a Chinese man. Jonathan started to struggle, until he heard the man whisper urgently in his ear. 'Get away from the carts. The attackers are fighting over your belongings. They won't see you if you go now.'

'My family,' Jonathan replied, trying to focus through the terrible pain in his head. 'I must help them.'

Together Jonathan and his unknown helper found Rosalind still in one of the carts with the baby and Helen. 'We must get away quickly!' Jonathan urged. Rosalind handed down the baby as someone snatched her hat off her head. 'Hurry!' their Chinese rescuer pleaded. Rosalind took off her shoes and threw them at a rebel who tried to snatch at Helen, grabbed the girl's hand and together they leapt off the cart.

The four of them moved as quickly as they could through the noise and confusion and headed into a valley. Their guide led them to a small village a mile away. He had relatives there who let them stay in a small mud hut near their house.

Jonathan's whole body ached as they laid him down on a straw mat. He was conscious of Rosalind giving orders to bring water and bandages, but he was too dizzy from loss of blood to be aware of much more. His last thoughts before falling asleep were of Paul and Ruth. Where were they?

Jonathan woke the next day, still in pain, but able to sit up. Rosalind smiled with relief, and started to tell him everything that had happened while he slept.

'Ruth and Paul are safe. No one was killed but poor Mrs. Cheng is very battered. She shielded Ruth with her own body when they were attacked. And Dr. Leslie can't walk. His back was injured. The carts are still in one piece and they're all waiting for us to join them. I'm sorry to make you move, but we can't stay here. It isn't safe for us or the village.'

Jonathan nodded and instantly regretted it. His head pounded with pain. But he made a determined effort to stand up and then said, 'Let's go.'

All Jonathan remembered of the next two days was jolting along in the carts, passing more crowds of sullen people. When they arrived at the great city of Nayangfu, the carts rolled through the streets until they stopped at an inn. Occasional stones and clods of earth landed near the carts and a few cries of 'Kill, kill,' were heard. They stumbled into the inn, with Mr. Mackenzie and Mr. Griffiths carrying Dr. Leslie between them. As Jonathan sat down heavily, he heard Rosalind pleading with the innkeeper for a doctor. The bandages on his arms were soaked through with blood and his head still felt like it had been used as a football.

The doctor arrived a few hours later. She marvelled that they had travelled so long without medical aid. 'There's no infection,' she said. 'But this blow to your head put a dent in your skull. How do you keep going?'

'Not by might, nor by power, but by my spirit, says the Lord,' Jonathan replied, reciting one of his favourite Bible verses.

Jonathan kept remembering that verse the next night when the whole party managed to creep out of the inn and into their carts. They decided to try to leave the city before it woke and avoid any difficulties with the crowds. But as the carts pulled out of the gate, Jonathan saw a flash of light on the hillside. More trouble! There must be men waiting for them.

Just then one of the carters rushed up to Jonathan. 'Stop the carts,' he urged as quietly as he could. 'Your son, Paul, and Mr. Griffiths are missing.' Jonathan tried not to panic. He instructed some of the men to come with him to check through the streets and back at the inn. He left one of the carters to protect Dr. Leslie and the women and children. Two hours later, just as the sky was beginning to lighten for the day, they returned without the missing man or boy.

'We must go on,' Jonathan told his wife sadly. 'Or we may all be lost. I'm sure God will take care of them.'

And so they began their journey again. Jonathan pushed away thoughts of his missing son now that they still had to face the ambush ahead of them. But God was protecting them. As their carts rumbled down the road, they saw their attackers. They were fast asleep on the hillside! None of them stirred and the entire caravan carried on to safety.

A week later they arrived in Fancheng more weary than they had ever been in their lives. Waiting for them was a message from Mr. Griffiths. He and Paul were safe and would join them at the river, where they would all sail to safety in houseboats to Hankow. Jonathan rejoiced that God had kept them safe. They were wounded and sore, but all had survived.

Devotional Thought:

*Indeed, we felt that we had received the
sentence of death. But that was to make us
rely not on ourselves but on God who raises the dead.
He delivered us from such a deadly peril,
and he will deliver us. On him we have set our hope
that he will deliver us again. You also must help us by
prayer, so that many will give thanks
on our behalf for the blessing granted us
through the prayers of many.*
2 Corinthians 1:9-11

The Apostle Paul wrote these words in a letter to the Corinthian church. He was telling them about a time when he had faced a deadly situation and his only hope was in God, who has all power, even to raise the dead. And God delivered Paul. But Paul also wanted the Corinthian Christians to know that they had helped with their prayers for him.

Later, when Jonathan and Rosalind read those words in Corinthians, they must have realised that their situation was much like Paul's. They had faced a deadly peril in China and God had delivered them. And do you remember when Jonathan was being attacked by the swordsman and others and he heard a voice saying 'Fear not! They are praying for you.'? God was reminding him that many Christians in China and in Canada were praying for him, knowing he and his family were in danger.

The Goforths' journey lasted for many more weeks before they reached a ship that would take them back to Canada. Jonathan recovered from his wounds and as soon as the Boxer Rebellion was over, he returned to China with his family. But before he went, he travelled to many churches in North America, telling them of God's deliverance and the importance of praying for missionaries.

Jonathan remained in China until 1935, travelling and preaching in the northern province of Hanon. He went blind in 1933, but continued working with Rosalind at his side, acting as his eyes.

CHINA

FACT FILE

China is the fourth largest country in the world. Shanghai and Beijing are two of the largest and most populous cities in the world. Beijing is the capital. Tienanmen Square, located in the Centre of Beijing, is the world's largest public gathering place.

It is officially the most populated country in the world. The Chinese Government has adopted a 'one child' policy in an effort to curb the high numbers. Unfortunately, this also makes China one of the fastest aging countries.

Mandarin Chinese is the official language. However in total, 55 official minorities and 206 listed languages are spoken.

The Chinese language has over 20,000 characters. The average Chinese only learns about 5,000 of these in his lifetime.

The Great Wall of China is over 1500 miles in length and is regarded as one of the Seven Wonders of the World.

China 1800-1900

BRUCE F. HUNT

B ruce was born in 1903 in Korea, the son of American missionary parents, William Brewster Hunt and Bertha Finley Hunt. When he grew up, Bruce decided to become a missionary too. He returned to the United States to attend university and seminary. After he graduated he married Katharine Blair, also the child of missionary parents. In 1928 they headed back to Korea to begin their own missionary work.

In 1936 the Hunt family moved to Harbin, Manchuria, to minister to the Korean Christians there. The region was under the control of the Japanese who had invaded and planned to conquer all of China. Soldiers were everywhere and the government issued many decrees about what people were allowed to do and not do. In particular, the Japanese wanted to control the Christian church and make everyone take part in their emperor-worship ceremonies. Bruce spoke out loudly against bowing down to the idols at the shrines. When the officials heard about him refusing to obey the law they sent police officers to follow him everywhere. Bruce knew it was just a matter of time before he would be arrested. Should he run and hide, or face being put in prison?

TO THE END

1941

The Hunt family had just sat down to breakfast in their dining room in the town of Harbin, Manchuria, when a loud knock sounded at their door. Bruce exchanged a quick glance with his wife Kathy at the other end of the table. Around them sat their five children: the twins, David and Mary, in high chairs, and three older girls, Lois, Bertha and Connie at the table. Suddenly the room was full of police officers. Three were Japanese and three were Korean.

'You are under arrest,' one of the Korean officers said. 'Pack a bag quickly.'

Before Bruce or Kathy could move, some of the officers announced they were going next door to arrest the other missionaries, Dr. and Mrs. Byram.

'Who's under arrest?' Bruce asked, worried that his wife and children might have to go to prison too.

The burly officer turned to Bruce and replied, 'Just you. We don't hurt mothers and children.'

Bruce gave a sigh of relief, even as his heart still pounded in his chest. He knew very well they would have no trouble hurting him. He thought of An Young Ai, a young woman who had been tortured the year before and had died rather than give up her faith.

Kathy told the children to stay in the dining room while she and Bruce went to the bedroom to pack a suitcase.

'You must take your warmest clothes,' she said, trying hard not to cry. 'And take your heavy coat and hat. Here are your fur-lined gloves too.' They both knew there would be no heat in the prison and it was the beginning of winter in Manchuria.

After she finished packing, Kathy said softly, 'I'm frightened, but I know God will take care of you and us. Let's ask if we can have family worship before they take you away.'

Bruce agreed and went to talk to the police officers who were sitting on the chairs watching the children play on the dining room floor. One of them was almost smiling, so when Bruce asked the favour of them, they said yes if it would be quick.

Bruce gathered his children around him, and Kathy came in with the packed suitcase. He took down his Bible from the bookshelf and read a short psalm. Then he prayed for strength and protection for himself and his family, and finally for the salvation of his captors.

'Enough,' the leading office said, and took Bruce by the arm. With his free arm Bruce grabbed his Bible and allowed the officer to lead him to the door. Kathy handed him his suitcase.

'Wait, Daddy,' Lois called and she dashed out of the room. Returning a moment later she stuffed something into Bruce's coat pocket. 'In case you get hungry,' she said.

'Thank you, honey,' Bruce replied as he was dragged out the door.

Bruce's last glimpse of his family was out of the back of the police car as they drove away from the house. *When will I see them again*, he wondered. Putting his hand in his pocket he felt two large chocolate bars he knew Lois had been saving for a special occasion.

Bruce was very thankful for those chocolate bars later that day. He and the Byrams had spent the entire day being questioned about why they wouldn't worship at the shrines.

'No one is stopping you from going to your church,' the Japanese officer said through his Korean interpreter. Bruce only spoke a little Japanese, but could speak Korean fluently. 'The law only says you must also worship the Emperor. Do that and you may go home again.'

'No,' Bruce replied, 'we can't. God has told us that we must not worship any other god but him and we must not bow down to images of anything. He is the only true and living God.'

Back and forth the debate went, with neither the Japanese officer nor the missionaries giving in. Finally, in frustration the officer ordered them out of the room and Bruce and the Byrams sat on hard chairs in a corridor. Since no one had offered them any food all day, Bruce reached into his pocket and shared the chocolate bars between the three of them.

Just as they finished some prison officials arrived. They grabbed all their suitcases and then marched them to the cell block, each led to a different cell.

'You won't need these,' one prison guard laughed unpleasantly, throwing the suitcases into a closet.

Bruce was going to protest until he saw the cell. It was already packed with every sort of criminal from all different nations. In fact it was so crowded that Bruce could hardly move once he was shoved into the cell. *How will we all lie down to sleep*, he wondered.

Then, without anyone saying anything, he watched them all begin to arrange themselves. Each man stood with his back to one of the walls and sat down. Then they all stretched out their legs to the centre, some overlapping with their neighbours. With a grunt one of them signalled for Bruce to sit next to him in a space smaller than Bruce's tall body. It was a tight fit but he managed to sit down too. He apologised to the man on his right who had oozing sores on his arms. Every time Bruce shifted he rubbed up against the man, who groaned with pain.

Bruce found the next four days very difficult. He couldn't sleep comfortably sitting up, afraid he would disturb the men on either side of him. His body became cramped and sore and he learned what it was like to be really hungry. Each man was given a small bowl of cooked millet and one cup of water each day. Some of the favoured prisoners received extra food, and the rest of them watched each bite those prisoners took.

Bruce learned that some of the men had been in this cell for over a year. He wasn't sure he could last that long in these conditions. *Please Heavenly Father, help me to be thankful for what I'm given*, Bruce prayed. *And give me courage too. I feel so weak.*

At the end of the fourth day the guard called Bruce out and handed him his suitcase and heavy coat and hat. 'Now, you'll need these,' the same guard informed him with a smirk, and pushed him toward the outer door.

Outside, the cold winter weather almost took his breath away. Pulling his warm coat around himself, he saw a line of prisoners, including his friends the Byrams and some Korean Christians from their church, all shackled together. Bruce was fastened into the queue with handcuffs and then they were hustled down the street toward the train station. People on the streets stood back and pretended not to notice the prisoners or the guards, not wanting to be anywhere near people who were in trouble with the government.

The long train ride took them south from Harbin to the town of Antung, near the Korean border. As they travelled through the night they couldn't see much of the mountainous region covered in a blanket of snow. But Bruce didn't care. He was more interested in speaking with his fellow prisoners than looking out the windows. They exchanged stories of their imprisonment so far, but more importantly those who were Christians read their Bibles and prayed together. The guards shook their heads but didn't stop them. One even seemed a little interested.

'My parents are Christians,' he admitted quietly to Bruce. 'But I'm not. It's much better to serve the

Japanese than be put in prison by them,' he explained with a little embarrassment.

'No,' Bruce replied. 'It's better to serve God. The reward in the end is much better. I have a home in heaven to look forward to. What do you have?'

The guard moved away quickly, refusing to speak to Bruce anymore during the journey.

The train journey lasted all night. At the end the prisoners were marched outside the town in the cutting wind to a large grey stone prison. Bruce could feel fear begin to creep into his heart as they marched through the iron gates. And it grew as he and the others were each put into single cells made of the same grey stone. Bruce had to bend over double to get through the small doorway. As the heavy wooden door slammed behind, he straightened up to find a small empty room with a high ceiling and one small barred window at the far end. A single light bulb hung from the ceiling. And it was bitterly cold.

How Bruce had longed to be out of that terribly overcrowded cell just the day before. But now that he was terribly alone, he almost wished he were back there. Instead of the constant moaning and grumbling of tightly packed fellow prisoners, all he heard now was the footsteps of the guard when he came near the cell door, or the occasional scream or shout from a prisoner being beaten in another cell. The only outside light came through the tiny window that showed a patch of sky. Inside the cell the light bulb burned all day and all night.

Bruce did his best to make the cell comfortable with the items his wife had packed for him. He had a change of warm underwear and socks and outer clothing. He used his fur-lined coat as a cover when he slept on the hard cold floor and wore his hat and gloves most of the time. Even still he never felt fully warm. Or fully fed. The rations came twice a day, cooked millet with salt radish and a cup of water. The water was necessary to get the food down. But as awful as it tasted, Bruce knew he had to eat to keep his strength and health.

All alone Bruce began to feel discouraged. He tried to keep busy, tidying his cell and doing exercises. But these didn't fill the whole day. He read his Bible, sang all the hymns he could remember, and started to memorise long passages of scripture. He was afraid that one day they might take away his Bible and he wanted to have as much of God's Word stored in his memory as possible. But even these things didn't stop the hopeless feelings that began to well up inside him. Would he just waste away here and die, forgotten?

Then one day as Bruce was pacing back and forth in his cell God gave him the words to a new song.

The words, *Give Thanks! Give Thanks unto Jehovah!*, suddenly came into his mind. As he quickened his pace, more words sprang into his thoughts:

For He of kings is King.
Let every nation, race, each tongue and tribe,
Unto Him praises bring.

And God gave him the tune too. Bruce began to sing as he paced excitedly now. Back and forth Bruce went singing the words that God gave him and feeling the discouragement melt away. Then he stopped. How would he remember the words? He thrust his hands into his coat pockets and was surprised to find a Chinese five-sens piece, perfect for scratching words on the wall of the cell. Bruce set to work immediately, carefully recording the words on the grey walls.

Over the next several days Bruce had scratched out six verses to the new song. The guard noticed it one morning when he brought the first meal of the day.

'What's that?' he asked.

Bruce was surprised the guard could see it from the small window in the wooden cell door. 'A new song that God gave me,' he replied. He sang the first verse for the guard.

'What does it mean?' the man wanted to know.

Bruce smiled. Not only had God given him a new song, now he was giving him an opportunity to use it to preach to his guard. The guard listened politely and then went away. That was just the first of many conversations Bruce had with his guards. All of them wanted to know what the strange American missionary was up to in his cell.

After what seemed many weeks Bruce was suddenly taken out of his cell. Once more he saw his fellow prisoners lined up in shackles. Bruce felt very scruffy. He had only been allowed one bowl of washing water each day and no razor to shave with. So his red hair and beard had both grown to shaggy lengths. But his fellow prisoners looked much the same. He joined the queue and was fastened to a young Korean man, who was hunched over in some pain. Bruce looked at him sympathetically. The guards must have beaten him. Then the guard jammed a necklace of tags over Bruce's head. Looking down, Bruce read his name and cell number on one tag and the number twenty-two on the other. *What did that number mean?* he wondered. Looking around he noticed his partner was wearing one too. Then he saw Dr. Byram with a number twenty-two tag and several others. Bruce smiled. Twenty-two must be the Japanese way of identifying the Christians in prison for refusing to worship at the Japanese shrines. It was a badge of honour. Bruce marched proudly with his fellow prisoners to the courtroom in another building. Once more God had shown Bruce that he was not alone. God was with him and so were his brothers in Christ. And God had one more encouragement for him too.

All through the day Bruce was interrogated by a Japanese judge who at first tried to get Bruce to change his mind by being sympathetic. 'Just sign the document that says you agree with our worship and we'll let you go. You don't even have to do it,' he said.

It was a tempting offer after so long a time in solitary confinement. But Bruce remained strong. 'No, I can't,' he replied.

Then the judge threatened him. 'You do know that if you weren't American we would be torturing you right now. Then you would sign. Should we torture you?'

Bruce knew that it was possible. 'I don't want to be tortured, but I can't betray God,' Bruce replied as bravely as he could.

Frustrated, the judge made Bruce sit for hours before questioning him again. But Bruce's answer didn't change.

The prisoners were exhausted and discouraged that evening as they walked back to the cell block. As they came near the wire fence Bruce noticed a group of women and children standing there, stamping their feet in the cold and blowing on their hands. When they saw the prisoners they began to call out in Korean. Bruce's partner looked up and smiled. 'That's my wife,' he whispered. 'Standing on the right.'

And then Bruce heard what they were all calling out to the prisoners.

'Gut ga jee! Gut ga jee!'

Bruce knew that meant 'to the end' in Korean. They were shouting words of encouragement to keep on going, persevere until the end. More words tumbled out, telling them that Christians were praying for them and that their testimony was being told to others.

Bruce returned to his lonely cell rejoicing. He, with God's help, would endure to the end.

Devotional Thought:

*He put a new song in my mouth, a song of praise
to our God. Many will see and fear,
and put their trust in the LORD.*

Psalm 40:3

David wrote this psalm to praise God for his help during a difficult time. God even gave David the words to write this psalm, not only to give honour to God, but also that others would hear the song and put their trust in God. Many people don't think about God as a songwriter. However, all creative actions have their beginning in our Creator. God gives the ability to write songs, play instruments, write stories and poetry, paint pictures and many more things. And a proper use of these abilities should bring honour and glory to God. The new song God gave David was for many to see and hear so that they would fear or respect God and trust him.

The song God gave Bruce was used to encourage him in his difficult imprisonment, as well as to tell his prison guards about God. Bruce remained in prison until the beginning of December and then was released. Two days later the Japanese attacked the American port of Pearl Harbor and America declared war on Japan. As a result Bruce was re-arrested along with many other Americans and was put in a concentration camp. Bruce suffered even more in this prison and almost starved to death. A year later he was released and reunited with his family and together they were sent home to the United States.

MANCHURIA

FACT FILE

Manchuria is a region (approximately 1,550,000 sq. km) in Northeast Asia which is today the northeast part of the People's Republic of China. The region borders Mongolia in the west, Russia in the north and North Korea in the east.

The region is the original homeland of the Manchu rulers of China during the Ming and Qing dynasties. Japan replaced Russian influence in Inner Manchuria as a result of the Russo–Japanese War in 1904–1905, and Japan laid the South Manchurian Railway in 1906 to Port Arthur.

Between World War I and World War II Manchuria became a political and military battleground. In the 1960s, Manchuria became the site of the most serious tension between Soviet Russia and Communist China. The Chinese claimed that the Russian seizures of Outer Manchuria in 1858 and 1860 were acts of imperialism and that Russian Manchuria should be returned to China. Despite exchanges of fire across the Amur River, tension has subsided and Outer Manchuria remains Russian while Inner Manchuria remains Chinese.

Manchuria in the 1900s

BIBLE CHARACTERS

You have now read four stories about men who lived in history. Even though they lived in different countries and at different times, they all loved God and took risks to serve him. As they studied their Bibles, those men read many stories about Biblical men who also loved God and faced risks. The next two chapters are about a man who challenged a powerful king and an apostle who spent time in prison. They chose to obey God, even when it was difficult and dangerous. They are good examples for us too.

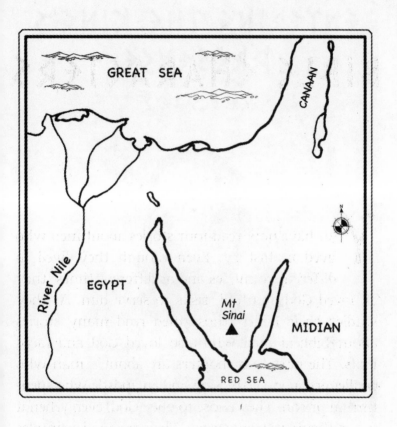

Egypt and Midian at the time of Moses

MOSES: ENTERING THE KING'S PRESENCE

EXODUS 3-12

Have you ever wondered what it would be like to meet a king or a queen? Would you know what to do or what to say? Today most kings or queens have only limited powers, so while you might be nervous to meet them, they are not likely to threaten you. But that has not always been so.

Adoniram Judson appeared before the king of Burma almost two hundred years ago. That was a dangerous thing to do. The king of Burma had power to order someone killed if he wanted to. There were no laws to protect people from the king's bad decisions. Someone in the Bible had to do the same thing. Moses had to face the king of Egypt to deliver a message from God. Do you think a king of such a powerful country as ancient Egypt wanted someone to come into his court with orders from God? Moses took a terrible risk to obey God's instructions.

Moses' story is found in the book of Exodus. It is such a long and exciting story, that it takes the whole book of Exodus to tell it, but we're only going to look at a small part of it.

Our story begins after Moses had grown up and was living in the country of Midian. He married the daughter of a priest and they had two sons. Moses became a shepherd, moving his flocks of sheep from place to place to find good pasture for them among the hills and mountains of Midian. This was very different from his growing up years in Egypt, where Moses had been adopted into the royal family and lived as a prince. At this point in the story, Moses probably thought he would live the rest of his life in Midian. But God had other plans.

God met Moses one day and spoke to him from a burning bush. It was a very strange sight to see a bush burning with flames of fire but the leaves staying green and the branches not burning.

And Moses said, 'I will turn aside to see this great sight, why the bush is not burned.' When the LORD saw that he turned aside to see, God called to him out of the bush, 'Moses, Moses!' And he said, 'Here I am.' Then he said, 'Do not come near; take your sandals off your feet, for the place on which you are standing is holy ground.' And he said, 'I am the God of your father, the God of Abraham, the God of Isaac, and the God of Jacob.' And Moses hid his face, for he was afraid to look at God. [Exodus 3:3-6]

Imagine how startled Moses was when he heard God speak to him! Moses was afraid, and with good reason. God is holy and good, and we are not. But God was gracious to Moses. He had work for Moses to do.

Then the LORD said, 'I have surely seen the affliction of my people who are in Egypt and have heard their cry because of their taskmasters. I know their sufferings, and I have come down to deliver them out of the hand of the Egyptians…. Come, I will send you to Pharaoh that you may bring my people, the children of Israel, out of Egypt.' [Exodus 3:7-8, 10]

God wanted him to go back to Egypt. Do you think Moses said 'Yes, I'll go right away'? No, he was not anxious to go back to Egypt at all. He remembered what had happened just before he left. The Israelites were angry with him because he was a prince while they were slaves, and the Egyptians were angry with him because he had killed one of the Egyptian slave masters. So he said,

'Who am I that I should go to Pharaoh and bring the children of Israel out of Egypt?' [Exodus 3:11]

Moses was sure no one in Egypt would listen to him, even if God himself *had* sent him. But God told Moses he must go, and not only that, but God told him the plan. Moses was to go into the palace and tell Pharaoh that he must free the Israelites and let them leave Egypt. Pharaoh wouldn't do it right away, but that was alright because God had plans to show all of Egypt his mighty hand and miraculous wonders. God did two things to help Moses. He gave him three signs to show the people and Pharaoh, and he also sent Aaron, Moses' older brother to help him. God promised to tell them both what they should do.

And so it was arranged. Moses said goodbye to his friends in Midian, and he and his family travelled back to Egypt, meeting Aaron on the way. Together they discussed what God wanted them to do when they arrived in Egypt and the huge risk that God was asking them to take.

Aaron was an Israelite and a slave, and had no business going to the Pharaoh's palace. The guards could easily kill him. Moses had run away from Egypt, from the palace and Pharaoh's anger. Although all these years later, there was now a new king in place. Would Moses be welcome in the palace? Would they still remember that even though he was born an Israelite, he had been brought up in the palace as a prince?

Moses and Aaron arrived in Egypt and did what God told them to do. They went to the Israelite elders of each clan, and told them that God had seen their distress and would rescue them. Moses showed the people the signs that God had given him: his rod turned into a snake and then back again into a rod; his hand became diseased and became well again; and water turned to blood.

And the people believed; and when they heard that the LORD *had visited the people of Israel and that he had seen their affliction, they bowed their heads and worshipped.* [Exodus 4:31]

How relieved Moses must have been. Surely Pharaoh would listen too. Or would he?

Let's just stop a minute and think about how God had carefully worked everything out up to that point. The Israelites (or the Hebrews) needed a leader and it had to be one of their own people. But he couldn't be their leader if he was kept a slave. So God arranged for him to be adopted by the Pharaoh's daughter. Moses then learned all the things Egyptians learned. Why? So that when he had to go into the palace to demand that Pharaoh let God's people go, he knew just what to do. Aaron may have been a better speaker than Moses, but he'd never been to court before. He didn't know how to speak to the Pharaoh, or what ceremonies had to be observed. Moses did.

So Moses and Aaron went into Pharaoh's court. Imagine what they saw as they came into the beautiful audience room. The walls were decorated with colourful murals, the marble columns covered with intricate patterns of gold and silk draperies moving gently as people walked past them. The Egyptian noblemen must have looked at them with their noses wrinkled. Instead of being dressed in fine fabrics, Moses and Aaron would have worn rough tunics and dusty sandals. This must have brought back memories for Moses of his growing up years. But he couldn't think about that now. He had a message to deliver to Pharaoh. After respectfully bowing to the Egyptian king, Moses said,

'Thus says the Lord, the God of Israel, 'Let my people go, that they may hold a feast to me in the wilderness.'' [Exodus 5:1]

But Pharaoh was not interested in what God had said. He replied scornfully,

'Who is the LORD, that I should obey his voice and let Israel go? I do not know the LORD, and moreover, I will not let Israel go.' [Exodus 5:2]

Pharaoh said no. And worse, he went on to accuse Moses and Aaron of stopping the people from working. So he said to the taskmaster,

'You shall no longer give the people straw to make bricks, as in the past; let them go and gather straw for themselves. But the number of bricks that they made in the past you shall impose on them, you shall by no means reduce it, for they are idle.' [Exodus 5:7–8]

Pharaoh had made the job even more difficult for the Israelites. They needed straw to bind the mud together. In order to make the bricks they first had to go and gather their own straw. Instead of the people being angry with Pharaoh, they became angry with Moses. They blamed Moses for making their work harder. If he'd only left well enough alone. Now their lives were twice as difficult.

So Moses turned to God and said,

'O Lord, why have you done evil to this people? Why did you ever send me? For since I came to Pharaoh to speak in your name, he has done evil to this people, and you have not delivered your people at all.' [Exodus 5:22–23]

Moses was feeling very hard done by. God had told him to give up his nice quiet job in the country and come to this pagan court to free the people. Instead of it all working out nicely, everything was now much worse.

But God had it all under control. He told Moses,

'Now you shall see what I will do to Pharaoh; for with a strong hand he will send them out, and with a strong hand he will drive them out of his land.' [Exodus 6:1]

So back to the court went Moses and Aaron. Pharaoh had to hear God's message again. 'Let my people go.' Even though God had told Moses that eventually Pharaoh would do as God had commanded, Moses must have worried that Pharaoh in his anger would order Moses and Aaron to be executed. Egyptians considered their pharaohs to be like gods and no one told *them* what to do.

When Moses and Aaron stood before Pharaoh the second time, he challenged them to work a miracle. So Moses signalled Aaron to throw down his staff and, just as God had promised, that staff turned into a snake. Imagine the surprise of the people in the court watching. But Pharaoh called in his magicians to see if they could do the same thing. The Bible doesn't tell us how the magicians were able to produce their own snakes, just that they did. But when they were about to say, 'See, we can do the same things you can,' the snake God had made from Moses' staff ate up all the other snakes. What an amazing miracle!

Surely now Pharaoh would recognize God's power and obey him, but no.

Still Pharaoh's heart was hardened, and he would not listen to them, as the LORD had said. [Exodus 7:13]

The next morning when Pharaoh, with all his servants, went to the river to bathe, Moses and Aaron were waiting for him. But before Pharaoh could command that his soldiers take Moses and Aaron away, Moses spoke.

'The LORD, the God of the Hebrews, sent me to you, saying, 'Let my people go, that they may serve me in the wilderness. But so far, you have not obeyed.' Thus says the LORD, 'By this you shall know that I am the LORD: behold, with the staff that is in my hand I will strike the water that is in the Nile, and it shall turn into blood. The fish in the Nile shall die, and the Nile will stink, and the Egyptians will grow weary of drinking water from the Nile.''' [Exodus 7:16-18]

And that is what Moses did. He raised his staff, brought it down in the Nile River and suddenly the water turned a dark red colour and became thick and very unpleasant smelling. What a shock that must have been! The Nile River was very important to the Egyptians. They used it for their drinking and bathing water. They washed their clothes in the water. They also needed the river for food. They caught and ate the fish that lived in it. Now all of that was gone.

It would be like having no water coming out of the taps in your house to drink or wash with, and no way to buy water either. Just imagine having to live a whole week without water. And not only that, but the blood and dead fish and other water creatures began to smell very bad indeed. It was a terrible seven days in Egypt.

Moses had hoped that Pharaoh would now listen to reason. Surely he wouldn't want the Egyptians to suffer anymore. But when Moses and Aaron went to see him in his throne room, Pharaoh was as stubborn as ever. So Moses delivered another message.

'Thus says the LORD, 'Let my people go, that they may serve me. But if you refuse to let them go, behold, I will plague all your country with frogs. The Nile shall swarm with frogs that shall come up into your house and into your bedroom and on your bed and into the houses of your servants and your people, and into your ovens and your kneading bowls. The frogs shall come up on you and on your people and on all your servants.''' [Exodus 8:1-4]

This time Pharaoh seemed to listen. After having to face frogs everywhere he went, even on his table and in his bed, Pharaoh called Moses and Aaron back into the court. He told them to ask God to take away the plague of frogs and then he would let the people go. Of course, Pharaoh was lying. He only wanted the nasty frogs gone. Then once more he refused to let the Israelites go.

Moses must have wondered how many things God would have to do to show Pharaoh who was really in charge. Would Pharaoh lose patience with Moses and Aaron? What would happen to them? Thankfully through these and the rest of the plagues to come, God kept Moses and Aaron safe from Pharaoh's anger. They were able to come and go from the palace, delivering God's terrible judgements for all to hear.

It took ten plagues to convince Pharaoh to finally obey God and release his slaves. By then the people of Egypt had suffered terribly and Pharaoh himself lost his oldest son. How foolish Pharaoh was. And how much Moses learned about God's greatness. God had given Moses an enormous task to do: to challenge a powerful king and free God's people. Moses took a huge risk to obey God and God took him safely into Pharaoh's court and then out of Egypt with the children of Israel.

Macedonia at the time of Paul

PAUL: DELIVERED FROM PRISON

ACTS 16:16-40

Prison is not a nice place to be, as Bruce Hunt found out when he was put in prison for refusing to worship at the Japanese shrines in Manchuria. While he was there I'm sure he remembered the stories of those in the Bible who also ended up in prison for their faith, people like the Apostle Paul.

Paul was the first missionary. He travelled to various countries in the Roman Empire, telling people the good news of Jesus Christ. The stories of his missionary journeys are found in The Acts of the Apostles in the New Testament. Paul had many adventures and took many risks to spread the gospel, and God used him to build up the early church. One of those adventures is found in Acts 16.

Paul was travelling with several other people: Silas, a Jewish Christian like himself, Luke, a Greek doctor, and Timothy, a young convert of Paul's from the city of Lystra. They had arrived at the port city of Neopolis in Macedonia, and then they walked along the Egnation Way, a wide stone Roman road. It took them up over the mountains and down into a large green plain where the city of Philippi spread out before them. Paul must have felt quite at home coming into the busy city with its marketplace, forum, theatres and temples. He had been in many cities before in his travels, and he had lived for a while in the city of Jerusalem. Whenever Paul arrived in a new city he would visit the Jewish people first, usually in their synagogue. But there was no synagogue in Philippi. So Paul and his friends set about looking for anyone who worshipped God, and they found them meeting outside the city by a river.

There were only a few women gathered for prayer, but Paul didn't care how small the congregation was. He just wanted to share the good news of Jesus Christ. So he sat down with them and began to tell them about the Messiah Jesus, how he had come to die to take away the sins of his people, and then came back to life again. The Bible tells us

One who heard us was a woman named Lydia, from the city of Thyatira, a seller of purple goods, who was a worshipper of God. The Lord opened her heart to pay attention to what was said by Paul. [Acts 16:14]

God spoke to Lydia, a wealthy woman, and she was converted, the first convert in this city with no Christians. She then offered the missionaries a place to stay, which they happily accepted. It was a good beginning. There didn't seem to be any risk telling people about the Gospel in this city. Or was there?

As Paul, Silas, Luke and Timothy walked through the city between Lydia's house and the meeting place by the river each day, a young woman began to follow them. She was a slave and rather wild-looking. But what startled the missionaries was what she began to say. She shouted loudly for all to hear:

'These men are servants of the Most High God, who proclaim to you the way of salvation.' [Acts 16:17]

At first Paul decided to ignore her. She was, after all, speaking the truth, although Paul knew she was possessed by an evil spirit. However, she was waiting for them every morning and continued to follow them and shout. Paul learned that she was owned by some nasty men who used her to tell people's fortunes.

They got rich, while she had very little. Finally, after several days Paul had had enough. He didn't want people thinking that Christians associated with fortune tellers. So when she wouldn't be quiet and leave them alone, Paul said to the evil spirit in her:

'I command you in the name of Jesus Christ to come out of her.' And it came out that very hour. [Acts 16:18]

But her owners were angry. She could no longer tell people's fortunes, and they could no longer profit from her. So the men turned on Paul and Silas. They dragged them into the marketplace, where people gathered and where the city magistrates held their court. The men accused Paul and Silas:

'These men are Jews, and they are disturbing our city. They advocate customs that are not lawful for us as Romans to accept or practice.' [Acts 16:20-21]

This wasn't true. Yes, Paul and Silas were Jewish, but they hadn't disturbed the city and they hadn't told anyone to break the law. A curious crowd gathered around the men and their prisoners, eager to see if there was any way they could be part of the action. The men turned to the crowd, encouraging them to beat Paul and Silas for their supposed wrong-doing, and the crowd joined in willingly. Suddenly it became a very dangerous situation. Luke and Timothy had been separated from Paul and Silas and could do nothing to help them. The Roman magistrates, aware how difficult it would be to stop the angry crowd, decided to agree with them. They gave orders to have Paul and Silas beaten and then thrown into prison. Paul was given no chance to speak in his own defence.

The angry crowd tore Paul and Silas' clothing from them and beat their backs with heavy sticks. Then they dragged the men along the streets to the prison. The jailor was not very kind to them. He put them in the darkest part of the prison, with no windows and a heavy door. He fastened their feet into wooden stocks, which meant they couldn't move their legs at all. There Paul and Silas sat on the hard, cold stone floor.

Paul and Silas could have spent the night complaining about their aches and pains, and the unfair treatment they had received. But instead of wasting their energy on that, they began to pray and sing psalms in the dark. Imagine what the other prisoners must have thought when they heard those two men singing in such a miserable place. They must have wondered what sort of men these new prisoners really were.

And it was a night for strange happenings. Not only were these prisoners heard singing instead of complaining, but at midnight,

Suddenly there was a great earthquake, so that the foundations of the prison were shaken. And immediately all the doors were opened, and everyone's bonds were unfastened. [Acts 16:26]

It was amazing! One minute every prisoner was fastened into his cell and the next, the whole prison began to shake. Chains fell off, the stocks released and heavy doors swung open. Suddenly the prisoners could go free! They could have run right out of the miserable stone prison. And that is just what the jailor was sure they had done.

The jailor of a Roman prison had an important job. He had to keep his prisoners from escaping. If they did escape, then he would have to pay for that escape with his own life. The jailor's whole family would be disgraced by his execution, so it was a terrible thing if the prisoners had escaped.

Paul and Silas knew all this. So they set about talking to the other prisoners right away. They persuaded them to stay in the prison. How did this happen? Well, it's possible that after listening to the missionaries praising God instead of complaining, the prisoners respected Paul and Silas and did as they asked.

From where Paul stood in the doorway of the prison, he could see the frightened jailor. He watched as the man drew his short sword out of the sheath that hung on his leather belt and turned it so the point pressed against his throat. The jailor was going to kill himself. Suddenly

Paul cried with a loud voice, 'Do not harm yourself, for we are all here.' [Acts 16:28]

The jailor's arm froze. The prisoners were still in the prison? Even after the earthquake? How could this be?

And the jailer called for lights and rushed in, and trembling with fear he fell down before Paul and Silas. [Acts 16:29]

These were the most amazing men the jailor had ever seen. He was used to dealing with criminals and people who were rough and crude. But Paul and Silas were completely different. The jailor wanted to know why. He wanted to be like them. So he brought them out of the dark, dank prison to his own house to speak with them.

Paul and Silas happily shared the gospel with him and his family, even though they still stood in their torn clothes, their backs sore and their bodies chilled to the bone. They ignored how they felt for the opportunity to share the good news of Jesus Christ. And when the jailor asked,

'Sirs, what must I do to be saved?' [Acts 16:30]

Paul and Silas replied,

'Believe in the Lord Jesus, and you will be saved, you and your household.' And they spoke the word of the Lord to him and to all who were in his house. [Acts 16:31-32]

In a night of amazing events, this was the best one of all! The jailor and his family were all converted. They believed in Jesus, knowing that only through him could they be saved from their sin and look forward to an eternity in heaven. What joy there was in that house when Paul baptized each one!

The jailor must have looked at Paul and Silas and realized that they needed care. So he had their wounds washed and bandaged and new clothing brought to them. Then he had a meal prepared and Paul and Silas sat down to enjoy some home cooked food.

Paul insisted that the jailor take them back to the prison after they had enjoyed his hospitality. He had persuaded all the other prisoners to stay, so he should be there as well. But what a different imprisonment this must have been. The jailor would have treated them kindly and they would have been much more comfortable.

In the morning the jailor visited them with a message from the city magistrates.

'The magistrates have sent to let you go. Therefore come out now and go in peace.' [Acts 16:36]

The jailor must have been pleased that Paul and Silas were to be released so quickly. And he must have been surprised at Paul's response.

But Paul said to them, 'They have beaten us publicly, uncondemned, men who are Roman citizens, and have thrown us into prison; and do they now throw us out secretly? No! Let them come themselves and take us out.' [Acts 16:37]

Paul was rightly angry. He and Silas had been treated very badly in front of the entire city. They had not been given a proper trial. And worst of all, they were both Roman citizens. The magistrates had no business treating a citizen like a criminal without following the laws.

A Roman citizen had special privileges in the Roman Empire. No matter where they travelled, they were protected by Roman law. Roman law said that a citizen had the right to a legal trial and couldn't be put in prison without one. And a Roman citizen could not be punished with beatings or torture. If any of these laws were broken then the citizen could report the magistrates to Rome itself.

When the magistrates heard what Paul had said they were frightened. They knew they would be in big trouble with the authorities in the capital city of the Empire. They might lose their jobs and their wealth, or maybe even their lives. And that was just what Paul wanted them to realize.

Paul and Silas waited at the prison for the magistrates to come themselves. The magistrates arrived with all their servants in front of a large crowd and publicly apologised to the missionaries for the bad treatment they had received. Paul and Silas listened as the magistrates then asked them to please leave their city. Paul agreed, but not before he visited with the small group of Christians that now met at Lydia's house.

So they went out of the prison and visited Lydia. And when they had seen the brothers, they encouraged them and departed. [Acts 16:40]

Paul and Silas had taken a risk to bring the Gospel to the city of Philippi. They, along with Luke and Timothy, had the joy of seeing Lydia, the jailor and his family come to believe in Jesus as their Saviour. But along with the joy came the unfair beating and imprisonment because they freed a slave girl from the grip of an evil spirit. However, that brought joy too. The beatings and prison were not pleasant, but when they praised God even in this difficult time, God heard them and delivered them, and filled them with joy.

WHAT NEXT?

S o, after reading all those stories, can you be a risktaker too? Have you got what it takes to serve God with courage? Could you choose to become a fugitive for doing the right thing? Could you risk telling someone very important that they ought to serve God? Could you go to a dangerous place and risk death or prison to tell others of God's love?

God might not ask you to do such dangerous things, but he does ask everyone who is a Christian to be willing to serve him no matter what. Could you risk losing friends because you chose to obey God's law instead of doing some mischief with those friends? Do you have the courage to say to God, 'I will serve you no matter where you want me to go or what you want me to do'? God is looking for us to have willing hearts to serve him even when it is difficult. And in the end, he has promised us a great reward.

WHO IS LINDA FINLAYSON?

Linda Finlayson writes the adventure stories of real people, bringing together her love of books, children and history. She has enjoyed working with children in schools, churches and children's clubs. Linda is a Canadian living in the suburbs of Philadelphia in the USA. She is married and has one son.

Linda has also written *Wilfred Grenfell: Arctic Adventurer* and three other books in the Risktakers series:

Strength and Devotion
Adventure and Faith
Fearless and Faithful

RISKTAKER QUIZ

William Tyndale

1. What was William Tyndale's greatest desire?

2. Where in Europe did he find a safe place to fulfil that desire?

3. What was the name of the English Merchant he stayed with?

4. How were the Bibles smuggled into England?

5. What did William Tyndale pray for just before he died?

RISKTAKER QUIZ

Adoniram Judson

1. What was the main religion of Burma when Adoniram and his wife arrived?

2. What dangers were there on the Irrawaddy River?

3. What change did God bring about after Adoniram and Dr. Price visited the Emperor?

4. Why was Adoniram sent to prison?

5. What did the Burmese Christians do to help Adoniram during his imprisonment?

RISKTAKER QUIZ

Jonathan Goforth

1. Why did Jonathan Goforth and his family have to flee from their home in China?

2. Where did Jonathan say the safest place was for them to be?

3. What did the Goforths do when they couldn't sleep at the inn?

4. What did God promise Jonathan as he was losing consciousness?

5. Where did Jonathan meet up with his son, Paul, and Mr. Griffiths?

RISKTAKER QUIZ

Bruce F. Hunt

1. Where did the Hunt family live?

2. What did the Hunt family do before Bruce was taken to prison?

3. Why did Bruce try to memorise as much Scripture as possible?

4. What did Bruce do with the Chinese five-sens piece he found in his coat pocket?

5. What did the women and children shout to Bruce and the other prisoners?

RISKTAKER QUIZ

Moses

1. In which country had Moses grown up?

2. What was Moses' job in Midian?

3. Why was Moses afraid to go back to Egypt?

4. What did God ask Moses to say to Pharaoh?

5. How many plagues did it take before Pharoah finally released the slaves?

RISKTAKER QUIZ

Paul

1. In which book of the Bible do we read about Paul's missionary journeys?

2. Where did the believers meet to worship God in Philippi?

3. Why were Paul and Silas thrown into prison?

4. Instead of complaining, what did Paul and Silas do while in prison?

5. What happened to the jailor and his family after God set Paul and Silas free?

RISKTAKER QUIZ ANSWERS

WILLIAM TYNDALE

1. To translate the Bible into English.
2. Antwerp.
3. Thomas Poyntz.
4. In sacks of grain and other goods.
5. The eyes of the King of England would be opened.

ADONIRAM JUDSON

1. Buddhism.
2. Pirates, crocodiles and snakes.
3. Missionaries were no longer threatened with persecution.
4. They thought he might be a spy for the English.
5. They brought food and encouragement, but above all they never stopped praying for him.

JONATHAN GOFORTH

1. The Chinese thought that missionaries had come to do them harm.
2. In God's hands.
3. Jonathan read the Scripture promises for that day and then they prayed for an hour.
4. 'Fear not! They are praying for you.'
5. At the river.

BRUCE F. HUNT

1. Harbin, Manchuria.
2. They had family worship.
3. In case his Bible was taken away from him.
4. He scratched the words of a song which God gave him on the wall of his cell.
5. To the end.

MOSES

1. Egypt.
2. A shepherd.
3. He had killed one of the Egyptian slave masters.
4. Free the Israelites.
5. Ten.

PAUL

1. The Acts of the Apostles.
2. By a river.
3. They had delivered a young woman from an evil spirit.
4. They prayed and sang praises to God.
5. They came to believe in Jesus as their Saviour.

GLOSSARY

American Consul: the office of the American Ambassador to China

Boxers: A group of people who called themselves the Society of Righteous and Harmonious Fists. Others called them Boxers because their training included boxing techniques and martial arts. They became anti-Christian and anti-foreigner, and in over two years they killed 270 missionaries and over 18,000 Chinese Christians.

Bread trencher: a small loaf of stale bread that has been hollowed out like a bowl to hold a stew. Once the stew was eaten, then the bread trencher was too. The part cut out of the loaf was eaten along with the meal.

Carter: someone who drives a cart and cares for the animals.

Cataracts: an eye disease where the lens of the eye becomes clouded by a thin membrane.

Doublet: A loosely fitted tunic that, in the 14th century, hung down to the knees. Usually worn with a belt at the waist.

Gold leaf: Gold that has been beaten into tissue thin sheets. It is used for gilding or covering an item.

Hose: stockings worn by men.

Magistrate: an important government official or leader.

Millet: a poor quality cereal prepared from the seeds of the millet plant (a tall grass).

Pith helmet: is a lightweight helmet made of cork or pith, worn as protection from the sun.

Sens: Chinese money coin.

Stocks: a wooden frame in which legs could be locked in place.

Viceroy: a governor of a province who represents the king.

Zayat: a small bamboo hut with a thatched roof. In Burma it is the traditional place people meet to discuss religious matters. Anyone who wants to teach religion builds one for people to visit.

Christian Focus Publications publishes books for adults and children under its four main imprints: Christian Focus, Christian Heritage, CF4K and Mentor. Our books reflect that God's word is reliable and Jesus is the way to know him, and live for ever with him.

Our children's publication list includes a Sunday school curriculum that covers pre-school to early teens; puzzle and activity books. We also publish personal and family devotional titles, biographies and inspirational stories that children will love.

If you are looking for quality Bible teaching for children then we have an excellent range of Bible story and age specific theological books. From pre-school to teenage fiction, we have it covered!

Find us at our web page:
www.christianfocus.com